1

POWER UP

Activity Book
with online resources

T0392228

Caroline Nixon & Michael Tomlinson

Map of the book

Hello

1 🎧 4.07 **Listen and number. Then colour.**

red	green	yellow	black	white
1	☐	☐	☐	☐

pink	purple	orange	grey	blue
☐	☐	☐	☐	☐

2 **Answer and draw.**

What's your name?

How old are you?

I'm Jenny. I'm six.

I'm _____ .

I'm _____ .

The Friendly Farm

1 🎧 4.08 **Listen and (circle) the number.**

1

2 (4) 6

2

1 3 9

3

2 5 7

4

4 8 10

5

5 7 9

6

3 8 10

2 **Write the words.**

1 3
t h r e e ☐☐☐☐☐

2 7
☐☐☐☐

3 9
☐☐☐

4 2
☐☐☐

5 1
☐☐☐

6 4
☐☐☐☐

7 8
☐☐☐☐☐

8 5
☐☐☐☐

9 10
☐☐☐

10 6
☐☐☐

1 Our new school

My unit goals

Practise	Say and write	Learn to say
	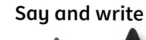 **8** **10** **12** new words in English	in English

My mission diary

	Hooray!	OK	Try again
1			
2			
3			
★			

My favourite stage: _____

Go to page 120 and add to your word stack!

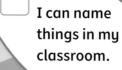

I can name things in my classroom.

I can understand colours.

✔ I can read classroom words.

I can answer questions with *Where ...?*

6

1 **Look and read. Write *yes* or *no*.**

1   The chair is purple.   _____yes_____

2   The desk is orange.   _____

3   The pen is green.   _____

4   The crayon is blue.   _____

5   The rubber is white.   _____

6   The bag is brown.   _____

7   The book is red.   _____

8   The pencil is pink.   _____

Sounds and spelling

2 🎧 4.09   **Listen and point to the letter. Then say and match.**

p or *b*?

p   b

 **1**    **2**    **3**    **4**    **5**

The Friendly Farm

1 🎧 4.10 **Listen and read. Who says it? Circle the name.**

1

| I'm the teacher. | (Gracie) / Cameron |

2

| It's under the desk, teacher. | Gracie / Rocky |

3

| It's on the desk. | Rocky / Shelly |

4

| It's next to the desk. | Gracie / Shelly |

5

| Where's my bag? | Jim / Jenny |

6

| It isn't in the bag. | Henrietta / Harry |

1 🎧 4.11 Listen and tick ✓ or cross ✗.

2 Look at the picture. Complete the sentences.

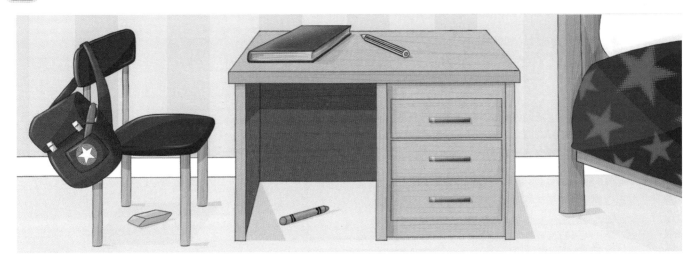

1 The book is __on__ the desk.

2 The rubber is _____ the chair.

3 The pen is _____ the bag.

4 The pencil is _____ the book.

5 The crayon is _____ the desk.

6 The bag is _____ the chair.

1 Write the words. Find the secret word.

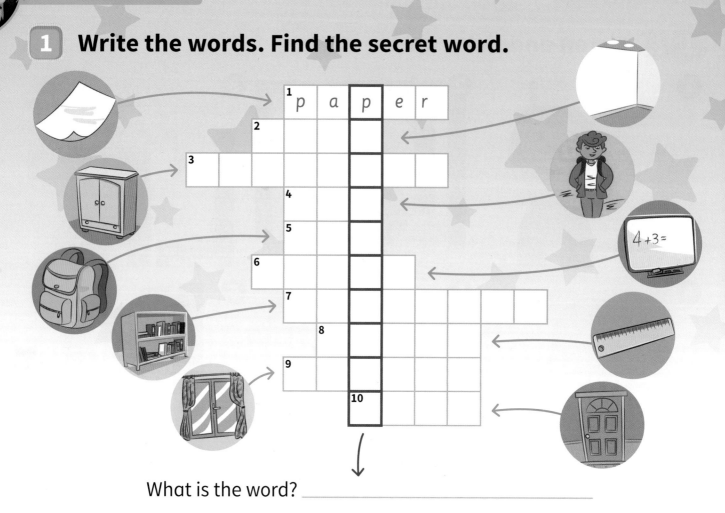

1	p	a	p	e	r

What is the word? _____

2 🎧 4.12 Listen and draw lines.

1 🎧 4.13 Listen and number.

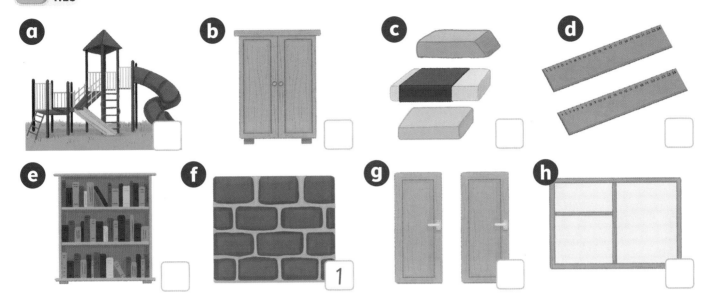

a **b** **c** **d**

e **f** 1 **g** **h**

2 Look and draw. Then write the words.

crayon   cupboard   It's   rulers   these   ~~this~~   this   window

1

A What's _____this_____ ?

B It's a _____ .

2

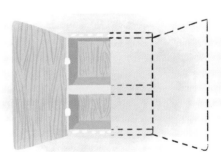

A What's _____ ?

B It's a _____ .

3

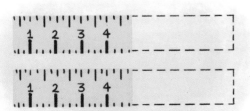

A What are _____ ?

B They're _____ .

4

A What's this?

B _____ a _____ .

1 Who is kind? Look and ⟨circle⟩.

2 Look and write the words.

Are you OK?   Here you are.
Thank you.   Yes, thank you.

Are you OK?

3 **How are you kind at school? Write the words.**

help   listen   ~~share~~   work

I ___share___ my things.

I _____ to my classmates.

I _____ my classmates.

We _____ together.

4 **How are you kind at home? Think and draw.**

1 🎧 4.14 **Listen and draw.**

2 **What do you take to school? Complete the rhyme.**

Take _____a pencil_____ to school – that's the rule.

Take _____ to school – that's the rule.

Take _____ to school – that's the rule.

Take _____ to school – that's the rule.

3  **Listen, point and draw lines.**

 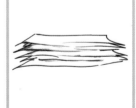   

4 **Look and point. Ask and answer.**

What's this? It's a bookcase.

What colour is it? It's green.

1 Look and read. Put a tick (✓) or a cross (✗) in the box. There are two examples.

Examples

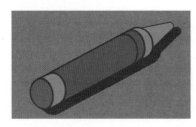 This is a crayon. ✓

 These are chairs. ✗

Questions

1 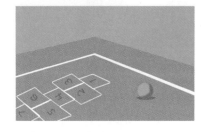 This is a playground. ☐

2  These are bags. ☐

3  This is a door. ☐

4  This is a pencil. ☐

5  These are rubbers. ☐

1 Play the game.

What's this? It's a rubber.

START

What's this?

What are these?

Where's the pen?

What are these?

What's this?

What's this?

Where's the book?

HAVE ANOTHER TURN

MISS A TURN

What's this?

HAVE ANOTHER TURN

What are these?

What's this?

Where are the rulers?

What's this?

MISS A TURN

What are these?

What's this?

What are these?

HAVE ANOTHER TURN

Where's the board?

What are these?

What's this?

What's this?

FINISH

What's this?

What are these?

Where's the paper?

MISS A TURN

2 All about us

My unit goals

Practise

Say and write

8 10 12

new words in English

Learn to say

in English

My mission diary

	Hooray!	OK	Try again
1			
2			
3			
★			

My favourite stage: _____

Go to page 120 and add to your word stack!

I can talk about my family.

I can listen to a song and do the actions.

I can name parts of the body.

I can read sentences about a picture.

1 Look and say.

Sounds and spelling

How do we say these letters?

2 🎧 4.16 🎧 4.17 Listen and repeat. Which words have these sounds? Listen and write *th* or *t*.

1 mo _th_ er

2 ca __

3 fa __ er

4 bro __ er

5 grandfa __ er

6 sis __ er

7 grandmo __ er

1 Read and tick ✓ or cross ✗.

1 She's my mum. ✓

2 She's my sister. ☐

3 He's my brother. ☐

4 They're my brother and sister. ☐

2 Who is in Rocky's family? Look and tick ✓ or cross ✗.

1 ✗
2 ☐
3 ☐
4 ☐
5 ☐
6 ☐

1 **Listen and follow. Draw lines.**

2 **Read and write.**

~~He's~~   He's   He's   He's   She's   She's   She's   She's

1    **2**    **3**    **4**

_He's_ Ben.   _____ Kim.   _____ Tom.   _____ Ann.

_____ a boy.   _____ a girl.   _____ a boy.   _____ a girl.

1 Find and circle the words. Then write.

①

head

②

③

④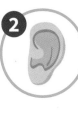

⑤

w	n	o	s	e	y	e	m
y	m	o	u	t	h	a	d
k	l	e	g	a	a	r	m
f	o	o	t	i	n	l	h
e	r	f	y	l	d	o	e
e	s	a	h	a	i	r	a
t	q	c	b	o	d	y	d
l	y	e	t	c	e	i	h

⑬

⑭

⑫

⑪

⑩

⑥

⑦

⑧

⑨

2 Write the words.

①

deah

_h e a d_

②

alit

③

byod

④

raih

⑤

tofo

⑥

sone

1 Look and read. Write *yes* or *no*.

Look at Hugo and Bill. They're cats.

1   They've got grey faces.   _yes_   5   They've got purple heads.   _____

2   They've got blue ears.   _____   6   They've got orange bodies.   _____

3   They've got red tails.   _____   7   They've got brown feet.   _____

4   They've got pink mouths.   _____   8   They've got yellow legs.   _____

2 Read and draw. Colour.

Hello. My name's Rob. I'm a robot. I've got a yellow body and I've got a blue head. I've got orange arms and I've got grey hands. I haven't got a tail. I've got green legs and my feet are black. My face is pink and I've got two purple eyes. I've got a grey nose and a brown mouth. I've got two red ears, but I haven't got hair.

1 **Look and write the words.**

hear   see   smell   taste   ~~touch~~

1    **2** 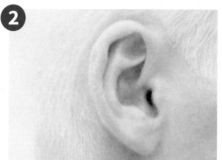   **3**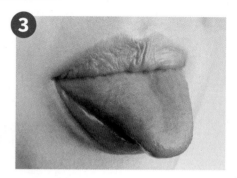

touch

4 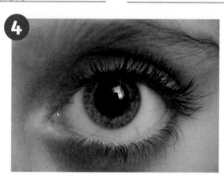   **5**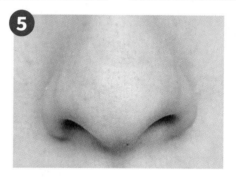

2 **Which sense are they using? Look and colour the T-shirts.**

 hear   see   smell   taste   touch

Learn about the five senses and sense organs

3 **Which senses do you use when you do these things?**
Read, think and tick ✓.

	I see	I hear	I smell	I taste	I touch
eat a sandwich					
watch TV					
play with a pet					

4 **Think of something you do at home. Draw it and tick ✓**
the senses you use.

1 Number the sentences in order.

a Sara is in the cupboard. __

b Sara is under the table! __

c Pablo and Sara play *Hide and Seek*. _1_

d Sara isn't in the garden. __

e Sara isn't in the cupboard. __

f Sara isn't next to the bookcase. __

2 Draw Pablo in the picture. Play 'Where's Pablo?'

Where's Pablo?

Is he under the table?

No, he isn't.

3 **Which body part can you see? Write the words.**

1

anhd

h a n d

2

deha

‾ ‾ ‾ ‾

3

ysee

‾ ‾ ‾ ‾

4

tefe

‾ ‾ ‾ ‾

5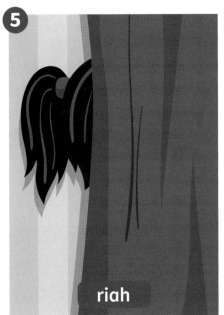

riah

‾ ‾ ‾ ‾

6

tmuho

‾ ‾ ‾ ‾ ‾

4 **Look and point. Ask and answer.**

What's this?

It's a hand.

What are these?

They're eyes.

1 **Look and read. Write _yes_ or _no_.**

Examples

Grandpa has got grey hair. _yes_

The pencil is on the chair. _no_

Questions

1   The cat has got white feet. _____

2   Dad is next to a desk. _____

3   Mum is reading a book. _____

4   The cupboard is under the window. _____

5   There's a blue ruler in the bag. _____

1 **Play the game.**

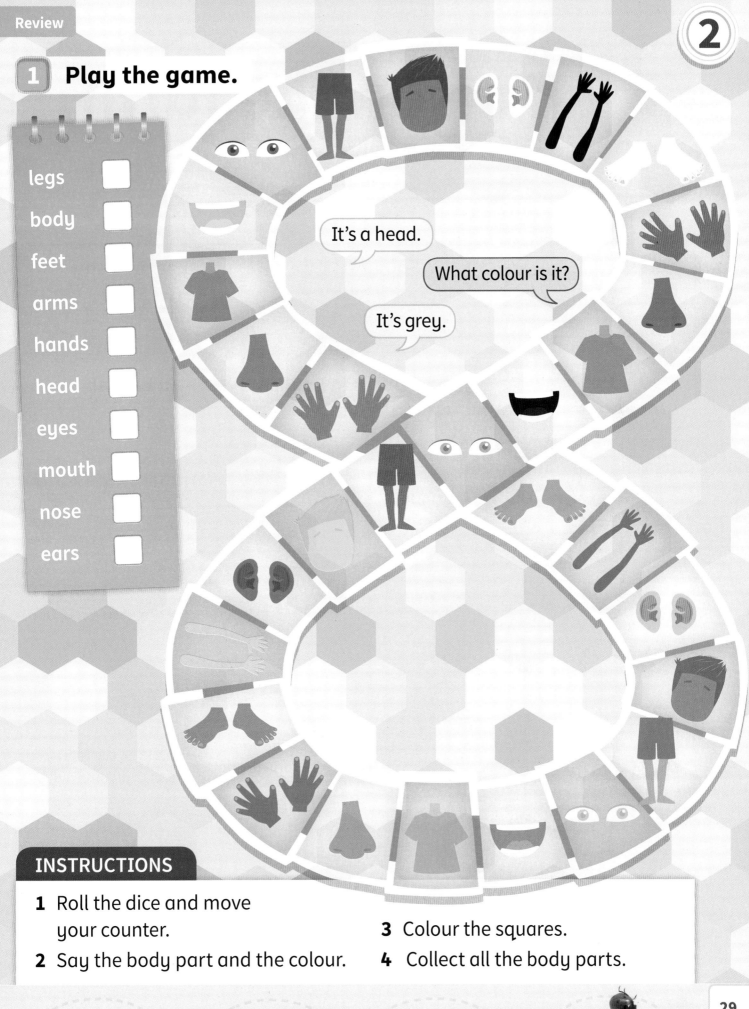

legs ☐
body ☐
feet ☐
arms ☐
hands ☐
head ☐
eyes ☐
mouth ☐
nose ☐
ears ☐

It's a head.

What colour is it?

It's grey.

INSTRUCTIONS

1 Roll the dice and move your counter.

2 Say the body part and the colour.

3 Colour the squares.

4 Collect all the body parts.

3 Fun on the farm

My unit goals

Practise	Say and write	Learn to say
	⭐ 8 ⭐ 10 ⭐ 12 new words in English	in English

My mission diary

	Hooray!	OK	Try again
1			
2			
3			
★			

My favourite stage: _____

Go to page 120 and add to your word stack!

I can name farm animals.

I can talk about animals and people.

I can spell animal words.

I can write about what animals give us.

1 Count and write.

cats   chickens   cows   dogs   donkeys
ducks   goats   ~~horse~~   sheep

I can see one ¹ _horse_ , two ² _____ , three ³ _____ ,
four ⁴ _____ , five ⁵ _____ , six ⁶ _____ ,
seven ⁷ _____ , eight ⁸ _____ and nine ⁹ _____ .

Sounds and spelling

How do we write that sound?

2 🎧 4.19 **Can you hear the /k/ sound? Listen and say *yes* or *no*.**

3 🎧 4.20 **Listen and colour the letters that make the /k/ sound.**

1    **2**    **3**

4    **5**

The Friendly Farm

1 **Read and tick ✓ or cross ✗.**

1

Rocky's new friend is a spider. ✓

2

Harry's a small horse. ☐

3

Cameron's a long cat. ☐

4

Rocky's brother and sister are old. ☐

5

Gracie's young. ☐

6

Cameron's short. ☐

2 **Talk about the animals. Use the words in the box.**

big   small   long   short   old   young   nice

Harry's big.

1 Read and colour.

The small horse is black.
The long pencil is blue.
The young cat is orange.
The big duck is yellow.
The new book is green.
The short ruler is purple.
The old cat is grey.

2 Write the words in the correct order.

1   short / The sheep have got / tails / .   _The sheep have got short tails._

2   spider / a small / It's / .   _____

3   nice / They're / ducks / .   _____

4   is big / horse / The / .   _____

5   cats / They're / old / .   _____

6   The donkeys have got /
    ears / big / .   _____

7   young / small and / I'm / .   _____

1 Read and circle the correct words.

1   It's a *sad* / (*happy*) cat.

2   It's an *ugly* / *beautiful* spider.

3   It's an *angry* / *nice* donkey.

4   They're *happy* / *sad* sheep.

5   They're *beautiful* / *ugly* ducks.

6   It's a *funny* / *angry* goat.

2 Write the words.

| angry   beautiful   funny   happy   ~~nice~~   sad   ugly |

1   This is the Mutt family. It's a family of dogs. They're n i c e .

2   The grandfather is _ _ _ _ _ _ .

3   The mother is _ _ _ _ _ _ _ _ _ _ .

4   The brother is _ _ _ _ _ _ _ .

5   The grandmother is _ _ _ _ _ _ _ .

6   The father is _ _ _ _ _ _ _ .

7   The sister is _ _ _ _ .

 **Listen and tick ✓.**

1 Which horse does Tom think is beautiful?

A  ✓

B

C

2 Who is May?

A

B

C

3 What's in Alex's school bag?

A

B

C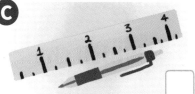

4 Which cat is under Jill's chair?

A

B

C

5 Which robot is in the picture?

A

B

C

6 Which animals has Dan got on his farm?

A

B

C

has/hasn't got   35

1 Which animal does it come from? Read and write.

bees   chickens   ~~cows~~   sheep

1 Milk comes from ___cows___ .

2 Eggs come from _____ .

3 Honey comes from _____ .

4 Wool comes from _____ .

2 Which things come from animals? Look and circle.

3 Read the sentences. Number the pictures in order.

1 This is an alpaca. It's got a lot of wool.

2 People cut the wool.

3 They make balls of wool in different colours.

4 They use the wool to make clothes.

a

b 1

c

d

4 What things from animals have you got at home? Think and draw.

1   Read the sentences. Number the pictures in order.

1   The flies bite Cathy.

2   Little Horse and Cathy jump in the mud.

3   The young cows laugh at Cathy.

4   Cathy is black and white. The flies don't bite her.

2   Read and write. Then write and draw.

1   Cathy is scared of _____ .

 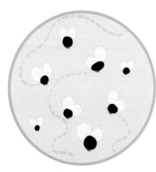  

horses   flies   spiders   mud

2   I am scared of

_____ .

3  **Look and read. Write *yes* or *no*.**

1	There are fourteen animals.	no
2	The animals are in a classroom.	
3	Cathy is a white cow.	
4	There are four sheep.	
5	There are four cows.	
6	The horses are smiling.	
7	Cathy's mum is looking at Cathy.	

1 **Look at the pictures. Look at the letters. Write the words.**

Example

<u>c</u> <u>o</u> <u>w</u>

Questions

1

_ _ _ _ _ _ _

2

_ _ _ _ _ _

3

_ _ _

4

_ _ _ _ _

5

_ _ _ _

1 Play the game.

START

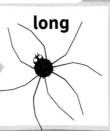 long

 new

 happy

 angry

 small

 young

 happy

 big

 small

long

 big

 old

 ugly

 short

 young

 long

 sad

 sad

 young

 big

 beautiful

 beautiful

big

funny

FINISH

 angry

 short

funny

 nice

The duck has got small eyes.

The duck is young.

INSTRUCTIONS

1 Roll the dice and move your counter.
2 Look at the picture and read the word. Say a sentence.

1 (Circle) the words.

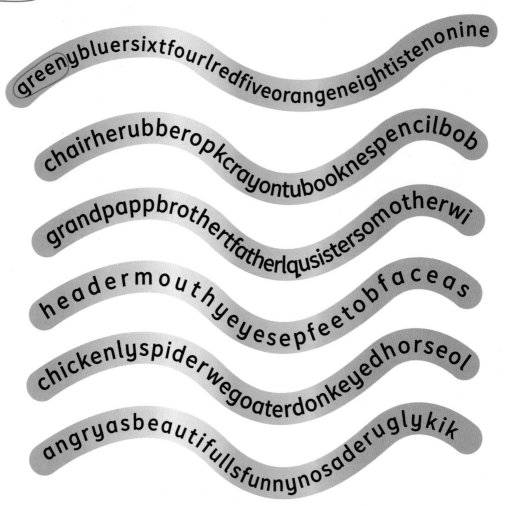

greenybluersixtfourlredfiveorangeneightistenonine

chairherubberopkcrayontubooknespencilbob

grandpappbrothertfatherlqusistersomotherwi

headermouthyeyesepfeetobfaceas

chickenlyspiderwegoaterdonkeyedhorseol

angryasbeautifullsfunnynosaderuglykik

2  **Listen and colour.**

3 **Ask and answer.**

	Name: _____	Name: _____	Name: _____	Name: _____
Have you got black hair?				
Have you got long hair?				
Have you got brown eyes?				
Have you got a cat?				
Have you got a dog?				
Have you got a ruler?				

Have you got black hair?   No, I haven't.

4 **Look at Activity 3. Write about your friends.**

1 Paula hasn't got black hair. _____

2 _____ has got _____ .

3 _____ hasn't got _____ .

4 _____

5 _____

6 _____

4 Food with friends

My unit goals

Practise	Say and write	Learn to say
	8 **10** **12** new words in English	in English

My mission diary

	Hooray!	OK	Try again
1			
2			
3			
⭐			

My favourite stage: _____

Go to page 120 and add to your word stack!

I can ask and answer questions with *Would you like …?* and *Can I have …?*

I can listen and write what food people like.

I can listen and choose the correct picture.

I can talk about food and drink.

1 Write the words.

 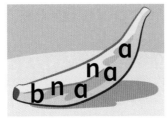  

1 ____mango____ 2 b_____ 3 b_____ 4 b_____

5 c_____ 6 c_____ 7 s_____ 8 w_____

Sounds and spelling

How do we say this letter?

 **2** 🎧 4.23 🎧 4.24 **Listen and say. Then listen and match.**

mango

cake

1 salad

2 cat

3 paper

4 lemonade

5 bag

The Friendly Farm

1 Read and tick ✓ the things Gracie likes.

I like cake, bananas, bread, socks and books!

 ✓

2 🎧 4.25 Listen and match the animals with the things they like.

 1
 2
 3
 4

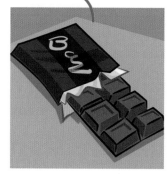

Story: *like / don't like* in context

(4)

1 Read and circle.

1   I *like* / *don't like* bread.

2   I *like* / *don't like* chicken.

3   I *like* / *don't like* bananas

4   I *like* / *don't like* lemonade.

5   I *like* / *don't like* water.

6   I *like* / *don't like* cake.

7   I *like* / *don't like* salad.

8   I *like* / *don't like* mangoes.

2 Read and match. Colour.

He doesn't like milk.	She doesn't like burgers.

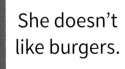

He likes salad.	He doesn't like cats.

She likes bananas.	She likes school.

1 Look and read. Put a tick ✓ or a cross ✗.

1

These are meatballs. ✗

2

These are oranges. ☐

3

These are sausages. ☐

4

This is fruit. ☐

5

These are beans. ☐

6

These are lemons. ☐

7

This is juice. ☐

8

These are grapes. ☐

2 Write the word and ask your friend.
Put a tick ✓ or a cross ✗.

1 Do you like _____ ? ☐

2 Do you like _____ ? ☐

3 Do you like _____ ? ☐

4 Do you like _____ ? ☐

5 Do you like _____ ? ☐

6 Do you like _____ ? ☐

1 Read and complete. Then draw and write.

~~bread~~ burger Can like Would

1

A Can I have some __bread__ ?

B Yes, here you are.

2

A Would you like a _____ ?

B No, thank you.

3

A _____ I have an apple, please?

B Yes, here you are.

4

A _____ you like some milk?

B Yes, please.

5

A Would you _____ some grapes?

B No, thank you.

6

A Can I have _____ , please?

B _____ .

1 Write the words.

carrots   cheese   meat   onions
~~pasta~~   potatoes   rice   tomatoes

1

pasta

2

3

4

5

6

7

8

2 Match the ingredients with the dish.

1
Ingredients
Fruit:
apple
kiwi
mango
grapes

2
Ingredients
rice
meatballs
tomatoes
peas

3
Ingredients
meat
potato
tomatoes
peas

a

b

c

3 Read the recipe and write the words.

cheese   ~~eggs~~   eggs   omelette   onion   tomatoes

1   You need two ___eggs___ , some cheese, _____ and an onion.

2   Mix the eggs. Cut the _____ and the tomatoes.

3   Cook the _____ for four minutes.

4   Put the _____ , onion and tomatoes on the eggs.

5   Fold the _____ and cook it for one more minute.

4 What would you like in your omelette? Draw and write.

I'd like _____ in my omelette.

1 **Find the words in the puzzle. Then tick ✓ the things Matt and Mia take on their picnic.**

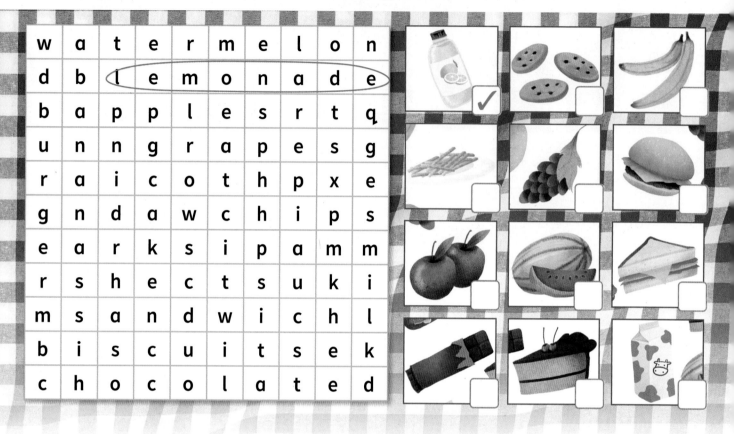

w	a	t	e	r	m	e	l	o	n
d	b	l	e	m	o	n	a	d	e
b	a	p	p	l	e	s	r	t	q
u	n	n	g	r	a	p	e	s	g
r	a	i	c	o	t	h	p	x	e
g	n	d	a	w	c	h	i	p	s
e	a	r	k	s	i	p	a	m	m
r	s	h	e	c	t	s	u	k	i
m	s	a	n	d	w	i	c	h	l
b	i	s	c	u	i	t	s	e	k
c	h	o	c	o	l	a	t	e	d

2 **Put the pictures in order. Then tell the story.**

a

b

c   1

d

 **Listen and draw lines from the names to the children in the picture.**

Matt   Mia   Tom

Tina   Sam   Harry

1 🎧 4.27 Look at the pictures. Listen and tick (✓) the box. There is one example.

Which is Bill's sister?

1 How old is Anna?

2 Where's Matt's rubber?

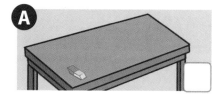  

3 What are the new animals on the farm?

4 What would Sam like for lunch?

 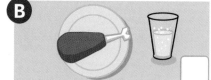 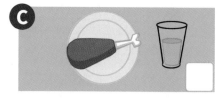

5 Which is Lucy's brother?

1 Play the game.

My shopping list

1 _____ ☐ 3 _____ ☐ 5 _____ ☐
2 _____ ☐ 4 _____ ☐ 6 _____ ☐

OPEN START SHOPPING!			Can I have ...?	

Can I have ...?				
				Can I have ...?
	Can I have ...?			
Can I have ...?				FINISH!

Would you like some lemonade?

Yes, please!

Can I have some oranges?

INSTRUCTIONS

1 Choose the food and drink for your shopping list.
2 Roll the dice and move your counter.
3 Collect your food and drink.
4 Go to the Finish! square.

5 Happy birthday!

Practise

Say and write

8 10 12

new words in English

Learn to say

in English

My mission diary

	Hooray!	OK	Try again
1			
2			
3			
★			

My favourite stage: _____

Go to page 120 and add to your word stack!

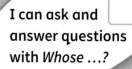

I can talk about toys.

I can ask and answer questions with *Whose ...?*

I can write a birthday card.

I can understand letters of the alphabet that I hear.

1 What is it? Look and write.

1

2

3

4

It's a bike.

5

6

7

8

Sounds and spelling

How do we say this letter?

2 4.28 **Listen and match the words with the pictures. Then listen again and say.**

a

b

c  1

d

1   house   3   horse
2   happy   4   hat

3 4.29 **Listen and say the rhyme.**

How is the **h**orse in **h**is little brown **h**ouse?

He's **h**appy in **h**is **h**at in **h**is **h**ouse with a mouse.

The Friendly Farm

1 🎧 4.30 Listen and read. Who says it?

Cameron	Gracie	Gracie	Harry	Rocky	Shelly

1 It's his favourite toy. _____Gracie_____

2 Whose car is that? _____

3 Jim doesn't like dolls. _____

4 Jenny's favourite toy is her car. _____

5 Look at our birthday present for Jenny and Jim. _____

6 Oh no! Not a plane! _____

2 Read and correct.

1 It's Rocky's birthday. _It's Jim and Jenny's birthday._

2 Jenny's car is orange. _____

3 Jenny likes dolls. _____

4 Jim's favourite toy is his bike. _____

5 Their present is a ball. _____

6 Cameron likes planes. _____

Story: Possessive 's and possessive adjectives in context

1 **Read and write *his*, *her* or *their*.**

1

It's Grandma and Grandpa's farm. It's ___*their*___ farm.

2

They're Harry's feet. They're _____ feet.

3

It's Jenny's car. It's _____ car.

4

It's Jim and Jenny's house. It's _____ house.

5

They're Shelly's ears. They're _____ ears.

6

It's Grandpa's tractor. It's _____ tractor.

7

It's Grandma's plane. It's _____ plane.

8

They're Gracie's eyes. They're _____ eyes.

1 **Write.**

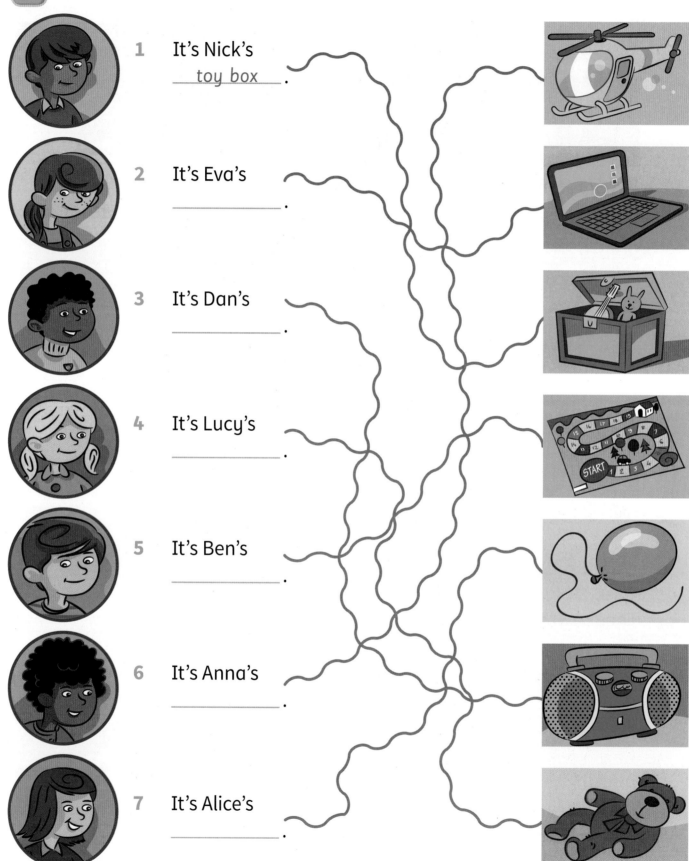

1 It's Nick's
toy box .

2 It's Eva's
_____ .

3 It's Dan's
_____ .

4 It's Lucy's
_____ .

5 It's Ben's
_____ .

6 It's Anna's
_____ .

7 It's Alice's
_____ .

1 **Write *Yes, she does* or *No, she doesn't*.**

Pat's birthday list

* a new computer
* a red kite
* a board game
* a yellow robot
* a big teddy bear
* seven balloons
* a small radio
* a green ball

1   Does she want a new computer?   Yes, she does.

2   Does she want a red bike?   _____

3   Does she want a board game?   _____

4   Does she want a yellow robot?   _____

5   Does she want a small teddy?   _____

6   Does she want eight balloons?   _____

7   Does she want a big radio?   _____

8   Does she want a green ball?   _____

1 Write the words.

circle   rectangle   square   ~~triangle~~

1
2
3
4

triangle _____ _____ _____

2 Which shapes can you see? Look and write.

1

I can see _rectangles and circles_ .

2

I can see _____ .

3

I can see _____ .

4

I can see _____ .

3 **Read and draw the robot.**

His head is a big square.

His body is a triangle.

His 2 arms are rectangles.

His 2 hands are circles.

His 2 legs are circles.

His 2 feet are rectangles.

His nose is a triangle.

His eyes are small squares.

His mouth is a rectangle.

4 **How many shapes can you find at home? Count and write.**

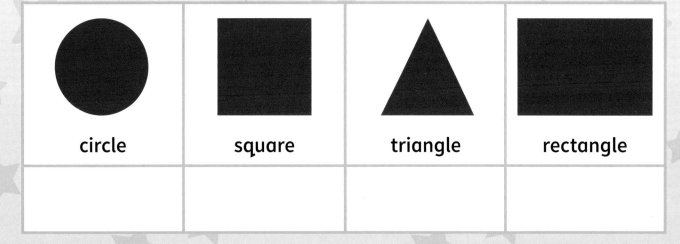

circle	square	triangle	rectangle

1 **Read and write *yes* or *no*.**

1   Dora and Cora are sisters.   _____ *yes* _____

2   Dora's favourite toy is a car.   _____

3   Dora's robot is called Jill.   _____

4   Cora gives her robot to Dora.   _____

5   Cora and Dora are happy at the end of the story.   _____

2 **Choose Dora and Cora's toys and complete the dialogue. Act it out with a partner.**

Dora: Can I have your blue _____, please?

Cora: OK. Here you are.

Dora: Thank you! Can I have your _____ too, please?

Cora: Yes. Here you are.
Can I have your red
_____, please?

Dora: OK. Here you are.
Would you like my
_____?

Cora: Yes, please!

Dora: Here you are.

Cora: Thank you.

3 **Cora and Dora share their robots. What do you share?**

I share my toy plane with my brother.

Look and read. Put a tick ✓ or cross ✗.

1

This is Cora's helicopter. ✗

2

Dora's got a red balloon. ☐

3

Dora's kite is blue. ☐

4

Cora's got a ball. ☐

5

Dora's got a car. ☐

6

This is Dora's teddy bear. ☐

1  4.31 **Read the question. Listen and write a name or a number. There are two examples.**

Examples

What is the name of Kim's doll?	_____Lucy_____
How old is the doll?	_____9_____

Questions

1	What's the name of Lucy's school?	_____ School
2	How many children are in Lucy's class?	_____
3	Who does Lucy sit next to?	_____
4	How many lessons has Lucy got today?	_____
5	What is the name of Lucy's teacher?	Mr _____

1 **Play the game.**

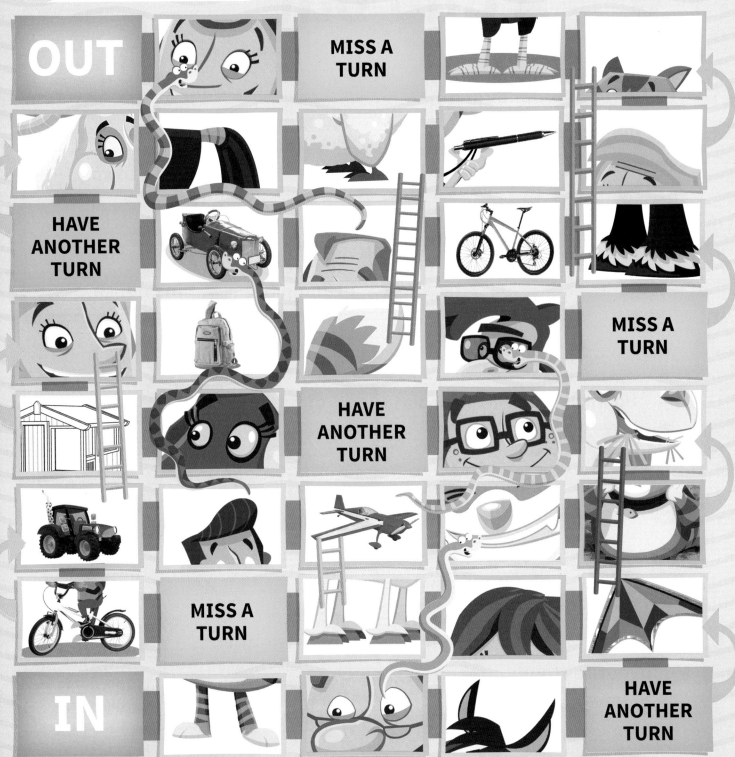

INSTRUCTIONS

1 Roll the dice.

2 Move your counter.

3 What can you see?

Whose is it? Look and say.

It's Harry's tail.

6 A day out

My unit goals

Practise	Say and write	Learn to say
	8 10 12 new words in English	in English

My mission diary

	Hooray!	OK	Try again
1			
2			
3			
★			

My favourite stage: _____

Go to page 120 and add to your word stack!

☐ I can name vehicles and places.

☐ I can talk about zoo animals.

☐ I can understand a poem.

☐ I can read sentences and copy English words.

6

1 🎧 4.32 Where are they? Listen and match.

1	cat	d	4	Bill	☐	7	Lucy	☐	10	Jill	☐
2	Dan	☐	5	horse	☐	8	dog	☐			
3	Alice	☐	6	Mark	☐	9	Hugo	☐			

park

garden

tree

flowers

bookshop

car

train

motorbike

bus

lorry

Sounds and spelling

How do we write that sound?

2 🎧 4.33 Listen and point. Then listen again and say.

3 🎧 4.34 Listen again and colour the letters that make the /eɪ/ sound.

train tail

cake plane
table grapes

1 🎧 4.35 **Listen, read and write the number.**

a   There's a big lorry.   _____

b   There are old cars and motorbikes.   __1__

c   There are flowers for Grandpa's new garden.   _____

d   Are there new animals?   _____

e   There aren't any new animals.   _____

f   There's a lorry and animals!   _____

2   **What's in the lorry? Look and tick ✓ or cross ✗.**

1  ✗   **2**  ☐   **3**  ☐   **4**  ☐   **5**  ☐

1 Read and colour.

Look at the street. In the street there's a purple car and a big blue lorry. There's a red bus stop next to the lorry.

Look at the shop. There are two trains in the window. The big one's green and the small one's brown. There's a park next to the shop. In the park there are three yellow flowers and a big green and brown tree.

2 Draw two more things in the picture. Listen to your friend and draw.

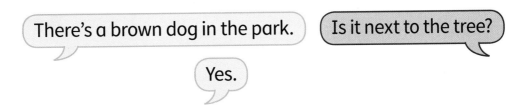

There's a brown dog in the park.

Is it next to the tree?

Yes.

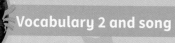

1 Write the words.

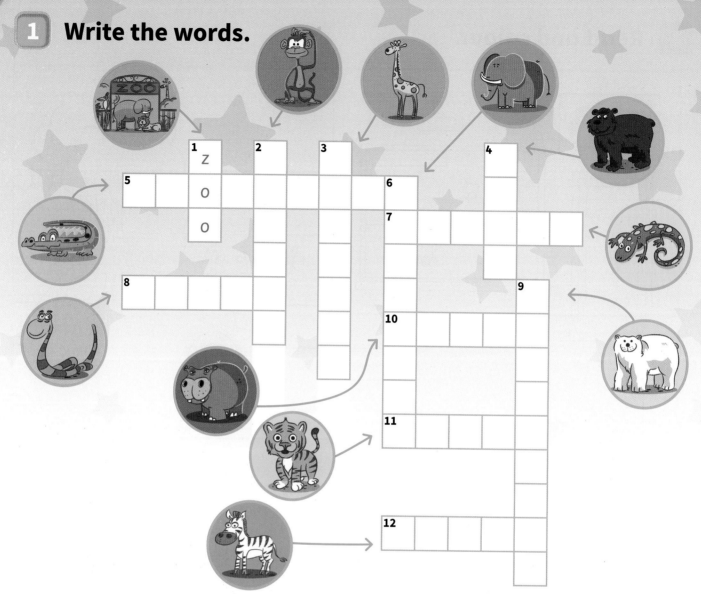

1 Z
O
O

2 🎧 4.36 Listen and write a name or a number.

1 What is the girl's name?   May
2 How old is the girl?   7
3 How many monkeys have they got?   _____
4 What's the small monkey's name?   _____
5 How old is the young monkey?   _____
6 What's Matt's father's name?   _____
7 How old is Matt's father?   _____

1 **Read and write the words.**

close   door   ~~game~~   Let's   Let's   listen

1

Let's play a _____game_____ .

2

_____ read a book.

3

Let's open the _____ .

4

_____ draw a picture.

5

Let's _____ the window.

6

Let's _____ to the radio.

1 Which animals live in the wild? Look and tick ✓.

1 whale ✓
2 zebra ☐
3 dog ☐
4 jellyfish ☐
5 monkey ☐
6 fish ☐
7 giraffe ☐
8 penguin ☐
9 chameleon ☐
10 polar bear ☐

2 Where do the wild animals live? Write the words.

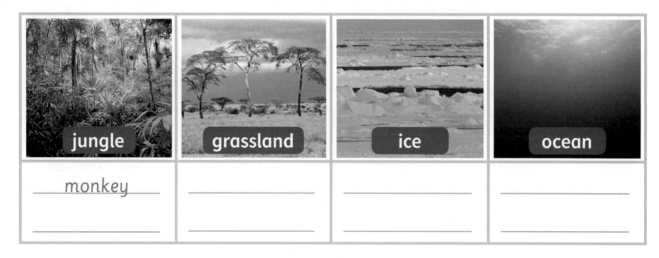

jungle	grassland	ice	ocean
monkey	_____	_____	_____
_____	_____	_____	_____

Learn about animal habitats

3 Read about the animals. Write the words.

big ~~frog~~ meat rhino small
snakes spiders trees water

This is a ¹ _frog_ . It is
² _____ and green.
It lives on land and in the
³ _____ . It can swim and
jump. In the wild, ⁴ _____
eat frogs and frogs eat flies and
⁵ _____ .

This is a ⁶ _____ . It
is ⁷ _____ and grey.
It can walk and it can swim
too. It doesn't eat
⁸ _____ . It eats
⁹ _____ and flowers.

4 Choose an animal to learn about. Draw and write.

• elephant • tiger • lizard • polar bear

This is _____ .
It is _____ .
It lives in _____ .
It can _____ .
It eats _____ .

1 🎧 4.37 Listen and number the animals in order.

2 Match the words that rhyme.

day   tree   ~~zoo~~   zoo

1 do ___zoo___

2 see _____

3 play _____

4 too _____

3 Make your own zoo poem. Write the animals that you like at the zoo.

I really like _____ ,
I like _____ too.
But I really love the _____ ,
When I go to the zoo.

4 **Listen and point. Then draw lines.**

5 **Ask and answer.**

What colour is the … ?

How many … are there?

Tell me about the …

Do you like … ?

What's your favourite animal?

What colour is the zebra?

It's black and white.

Tell me about the elephant.

It's big and grey.

1 Read this. Choose a word from the box. Write the correct word next to numbers 1–5. There is one example.

A zebra

Zebras are _____black_____ and white animals. They are like horses but people don't ride them. A zebra's **(1)** _____ is nice and long. A zebra has got four legs and two beautiful **(2)** _____. Lots of zebras live with their family. Some zebras live in the **(3)** _____. Zebras drink a lot of **(4)** _____, but they don't eat **(5)** _____.

Example

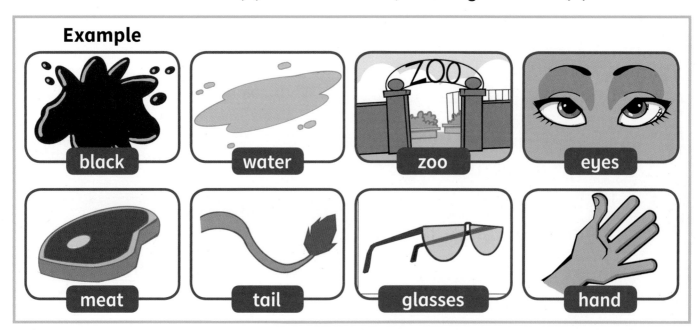

black   water   zoo   eyes

meat   tail   glasses   hand

1 Play the game.

There are two hippos next to a bus stop.

FINISH

There's a zebra under the tree.

There are two monkeys in the helicopter.

There's a bear in the shop.

There's a crocodile on the motorbike.

There are three flowers on the lorry.

START

There are two trees in the park.

There are two trees in the park.

INSTRUCTIONS

1 Roll the dice.
2 Move your counter.

3 Pictures: Say what you see.
4 Sentences: Read, find and move to that square.

1 **Find three words in a line from the same group.**

1

doll	tree	flower
street	balloon	board game
computer	salad	kite

2

sausage	lizard	bike
beans	polar bear	lorry
giraffe	tiger	burger

3

bread	mango	lorry
radio	train	bear
motorbike	teddy	apple

4

park	house	chocolate
water	shop	chicken
garden	donkey	meat

2 🎧 4.39 **Listen and colour.**

3 Read and match. Colour

 **1** ✓

 **2** ✗

 **3** ✓

 **4** ✓

 **5** ✗

 **6** ✗

They want a board game.

He doesn't want any grapes.

He wants some orange juice.

She wants some bananas.

They don't want a teddy.

She doesn't want a beautiful doll.

4 Write.

beans̶ bear cake crocodile dog helicopter
kite lizard lorry meat plane robot

food	transport	wild animals	other
beans			

7 Let's play

My unit goals

Practise	Say and write	Learn to say
	8 10 12	
	new words in English	in English

My mission diary

	Hooray!	OK	Try again
1			
2			
3			
★			

My favourite stage: _____

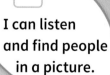

Go to page 120 and add to your word stack!

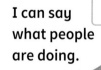

I can talk about hobbies.

I can say what people are doing.

I can listen and find people in a picture.

I can understand questions with *Can I …?*

1 Read and match.

a — Let's play basketball.

b — Let's play the piano.

c — Let's play football.

d — Let's swim.

e — Let's watch television.

f — Let's play tennis.

g — Let's ride our bikes.

h — Let's play the guitar.

Sounds and spelling

2 🎧 4.40 **Listen and say the rhyme.**

My **s**i**s**ter **S**ally like**s** **s**alad and **s**wimming, but I like **s**pider**s**, **s**au**s**age**s** and **s**nake**s**!

How do we say this letter?

1 **Read and (circle) the correct word.**

Tom's *(riding)* / *watching* Harry.

Rocky's brother and sister are *singing* / *eating*.

She's eating a *book* / *sock*.

She's painting her *face* / *feet*.

Rocky says he's playing *the guitar* / *the piano*.

Henrietta's *cleaning* / *painting* the barn.

2 **Look and talk about the people and animals. Use the words in the box.**

watching   riding   talking   walking   singing   smiling

Mr Friendly is watching Tom and Harry.

1 Look and read. Write *yes* or *no*.

1 The girl's driving a car. _no_

2 The baby's running. _____

3 The boy's playing tennis. _____

4 The mother's painting a picture. _____

5 The father's playing the guitar. _____

6 The grandfather's listening
to music. _____

2 Look and write the words.

am ~~are~~ aren't is isn't

A What _are_ you doing?

B I _____ listening to music.

A Are they playing basketball?

B No, they _____ .

A Is your mum watching TV?

B No, she _____ . She's reading.

A What's he doing?

B He _____ playing the guitar.

1 Look and write the words.

badminton   baseball   basketball   hitting
~~hockey~~   kicking   running   skateboard

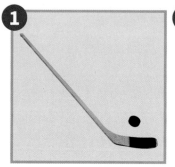

1. hockey

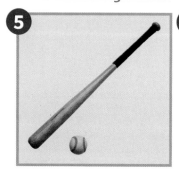

2  Listen and colour.

4.41

1 Write the words in the correct order.

1

our skateboards / in the park / Can we ride / ?

Can we ride our skateboards

in the park?

2

Can I throw / your dog / the ball for / ?

3

please / eat some cake, / Can we / ?

4

the train, / Can we go on / please / ?

5

Can I / please / watch television, / ?

6

badminton in / the garden / Can we play / ?

1 **Play a mime game. Do and say.**

jump   run   stretch your legs
stretch your arms   stretch your body

What am I doing?   You're jumping.

2 **What are they doing?
Look, read and write.**

1   _____Alice_____ is stretching her body.

2   _____ is stretching his legs.

3   _____ is stretching her arms.

4   Sam is _____.

5   Grace is _____.

Learn about how we can keep our bodies strong

3 **Who is looking after their bodies? Look and tick ✓.**

4 **How do you look after your body? Draw and write.**

1 **Talk about what you think happens next in the story.**

I think Oliver plays with the big boys.   I think Oliver plays with Alfie.

2 **Draw the next picture in the story.**

3 **Look at your drawing. Write a conversation.**

Oliver: *Thank you, Alfie.* _____

Alfie: _____

_____

_____

_____

4 **Act out the conversation.**

Thank you, Alfie.   That's OK.

5  **Listen and tick ✓.**

1 What has Alfie got?

A ✓

B

C

2 How old is Amelia?

A

B

C

3 What is Oliver doing now?

A

B

C

4 How is Amelia today?

A

B

C

5 Where's Oliver's skateboard?

A

B

C

6 What would Alfie like to eat?

A

B

C

1 🎧 **Listen and draw lines. There is one example.**
4.43

Matt   Nick   Grace   Sam

Tom   May   Eva

1 Play the game.

INSTRUCTIONS

1 Roll the dice and move your counter.
2 Say what the people and animals are doing.

What's he doing?

He's riding a bike.

My unit goals

Practise

Say and write

8 10 12

new words in English

Learn to say

in English

My mission diary

	Hooray!	OK	Try again
1	😊	😐	😕
2	😊	😐	😟
3	😊	😐	😕
⭐	😊	😐	😟

My favourite stage: _____

Go to page 120 and add to your word stack!

I can name rooms and things in the house.

I can talk about what I can and can't do.

I can listen and colour a picture.

I can listen and understand where things are.

1 🎧 4.44 Listen and tick ✓ or cross ✗.

1 ✗

2

3

4

5

6

Sounds and spelling

2 🎧 4.45 🎧 4.46 Listen and say. Then listen and match.

How do we say this letter?

living room

dining room

1 lizard

2 mirror

3 kite

4 tiger

5 ship

6 bike

The Friendly Farm

1 🎧 4.47 **Listen, read and tick ✓ or cross ✗.**

1

Rocky can ride a horse. ✓

2

Shelly can't sing. ☐

3

Rocky's brother and sister can't swim. ☐

4

Harry can swim. ☐

5

Rocky can dance. ☐

6

Rocky can eat books. ☐

2 **What can you do? Look and say.**

I can sing but I can't eat books!

Story: *can* for ability in context

1 🎧 4.48 Listen and join. Then write.

 **1** Hugo
 **2** Sam
 **3** Pat
 **4** May
 **5** Tony
 **6** Alex

 **a**
 **b**
 **c**
 **d**
 **e**
 **f**

1 Hugo can play tennis.

2 _____

3 _____

4 _____

5 _____

6 _____

2 Answer the questions. Write *Yes, I can* and *No, I can't.*

All about me

1 Can you ride a bike? _____

2 Can you play the guitar? _____

3 Can you swim? _____

4 Can you play table tennis? _____

5 Can you sing? _____

6 Can you play football? _____

7 Can you draw? _____

8 Can you ride a horse? _____

1 **Find and circle the words. Then say.**

w	y	s	p	q	s	a	j	l
p	h	o	n	e	t	r	g	b
o	z	f	n	c	m	m	k	e
j	q	a	w	l	e	c	z	d
m	i	r	r	o	r	h	g	v
h	x	u	j	c	l	a	m	p
r	t	g	z	k	g	i	j	r
v	b	l	f	x	o	r	e	q
k	r	p	h	o	t	o	k	i

Number 1 is a photo.

2 **Look at the picture and read the questions. Write one-word answers.**

1   Where is the girl?

on the ___sofa___

2   Who is listening to music?

the _____

3   Where are the girl and boy?

in the _____ room

4   What's the girl doing?

watching _____

5   Where's the boy sitting?

on the _____

6   What colour's the wall? _____

7   What's their dad cleaning?

the _____

1 Read and draw lines.

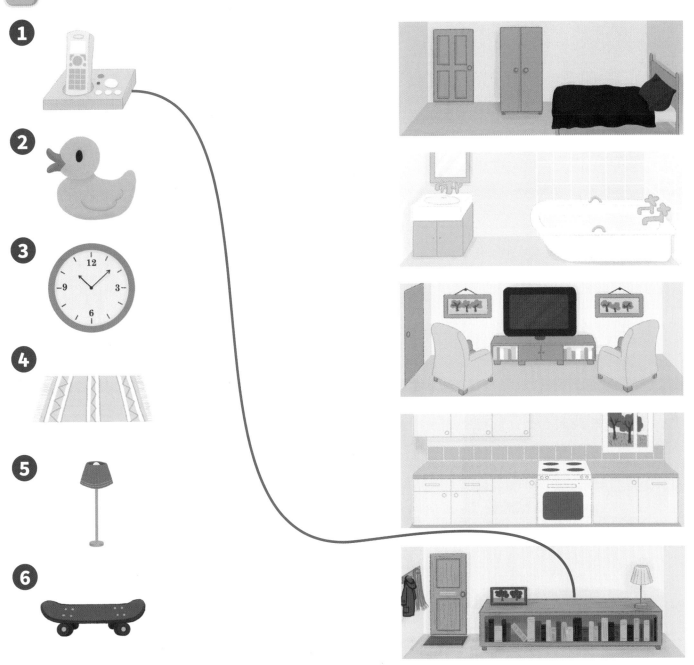

The phone is between the photo and the lamp in the hall.

The duck is in front of the bath in the bathroom.

The clock is in the kitchen. It's between the window and the cupboard.

The rug is on the floor in front of the television in the living room.

The lamp is behind the armchair in the living room.

The skateboard is in the bedroom. It's between the door and the cupboard.

1 Write the words.

```
      1
      s
3         t i l t
      i
      l
4         t
      6 h
      o
      u
      s
      e
```

Learn about different kinds of houses around the world

2 Read and match.

 **a**

 **b**

 **c**

 **1** I've got a treehouse in my garden and sometimes I sleep there. It's called a treehouse because it's in the trees! In the morning I can hear the birds. It's great!

 **2** I live in Vietnam. The houses in my village are lots of different colours and they are all on the water. I like it because we can swim and catch fish.

 **3** My house has got four rooms – a living room, a kitchen, a bathroom and two bedrooms. How is my house different? It moves! I like it because we can go to different places and take our house with us.

3 Think about the house you want to live in. Draw and write.

1 **Read and write the words.**

> ~~ball~~   bath   bounce   clock   OK   table

1   Rob finds a ____ball____ .

2   Rob and Sue throw and catch and _____ the ball.

3   The ball bounces in the _____ and on the sofa.

4   The ball bounces on the _____ and on the chair.

5   The _____ falls on the mat.

6   Sue says that the clock is _____ .

2 **Sue and Rob play with the ball in the house. That isn't a good idea! What can you do with your friends in the house? What can you do in the garden?**

> We can play board games in the house.

> We can play football in the garden.

3 Look at the pictures and read the questions. Write one-word answers.

1 Where are the children?

in Sue's _____bedroom_____

2 What are they doing?

playing with _____

3 Where is the yellow car?

on the _____

4 What is Rob pointing to?

the red _____

5 Who has got the yellow car?

_____

6 Where is the yellow car now?

under the _____

7 Who has got the red car?

_____

1 🎧 4.49 Listen and colour. There is one example.

8

1 Play the game.

You're watching television in the living room.
Miss a turn.

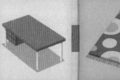

a bed ☐
a lamp ☐
an armchair ☐
a phone ☐
a desk ☐
a mat ☐
a cupboard ☐
a photo ☐
a clock ☐
a mirror ☐

You're singing in the bath.
Miss a turn.

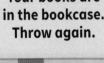

Your books are in the bookcase.
Throw again.

Your bedroom is clean.
Throw again.

What have you got?

I've got a lamp for my bedroom.

INSTRUCTIONS

1 Start in the bedroom.
2 Roll the dice and move your counter.
3 Collect all the objects.
4 Go back to your bedroom.

9 Happy holidays

My unit goals

Practise	Say and write new words in English	Learn to say in English

My mission diary

	Hooray!	OK	Try again
1			
2			
3			
★			

My favourite stage: _____

Go to page 120 and add to your word stack!

I can name clothes.

I can understand instructions.

I can talk about things at the beach.

I can read and answer questions about a picture story.

1 **Look and read. Write *yes* or *no*.**

1

This is a hat.
yes

2

These are socks.

3
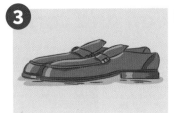
These are shoes.

4

This is a skirt.

5

This is a jacket.

6

These are glasses.

7

These are jeans.

8

This is a T-shirt.

Sounds and spelling

2 🎧 4.50 **Listen and point to the letter.
Then say, match and write the letter.**

j or h?

 j

 h

1  j eans

2 __and

3 __at

4 __uice

5 __orse

6 __acket

7 __ippo

1 🎧 4.51 **Listen, read and correct.**

That's Grandpa's
new ~~shirt~~!
_____ hat

Let's go and eat
in the barn.
_____

Come here and pick up
these toys, please!
_____

Now clean the mirror,
Gracie. It's dirty.
_____

Take those pencils and
put them in the box.
_____

Grandpa's hat's there
on the sofa.
_____

2 **Act it out with a partner. Say and do. Use the words in the box.**

> pick up   clean   take   put   come

> Pick up those pencils, please.

1 Look, read and write the number.

1

1 Anna, pick up that jacket, please.

2 Put the ball in that cupboard there, please.

3 Take this book to the bookcase, please.

4 Pick up those trousers, please.

5 Put these bananas on that table, there, please.

6 OK, children, clean these desks, please.

2 Write the words.

boots   ~~read~~   sunglasses   trousers

1

Let's _____read_____ these books.

2

Are these your _____?

3

Clean those _____.

4

Those aren't your _____.

1 **Find and circle the words. Then write.**

shell

s	h	e	l	l	q	h	o	p	l	n
j	u	c	v	r	i	s	h	l	n	g
e	z	n	g	b	e	a	c	h	e	l
l	b	n	g	u	w	n	d	a	c	m
l	i	k	w	l	c	d	k	e	r	n
y	t	a	k	e	a	p	h	o	t	o
f	i	s	h	m	m	s	e	a	t	u
i	z	h	k	h	e	t	s	w	s	i
s	u	n	l	t	r	o	y	e	p	g
h	b	o	a	t	a	j	w	b	s	h

2 **Read and colour.**

Kim's at the beach. She's sitting on the yellow sand. She's got a purple camera and she's taking a photo of a big pink shell, next to her. She's got some big green sunglasses on her head. There's an orange boat on the blue sea. It's got a big red fish on it. There's a man in the boat. He's fishing.

1 Read and write the words.

The beach

A lot of people like going to the ___beach___ on holiday. You can wear a
(1) _____ and shorts and you can do different things there.

Some people enjoy sitting in the sun, reading a book or listening to the
(2) _____. Children like playing on the sand. They can pick up
(3) _____ and write their names with them.

A lot of people enjoy swimming in the **(4)** _____. They can look at
(5) _____ and shells under the water.

beach	sea	boots	radio
camera	fish	shells	T-shirt

1 **Write the words.**

beach   forest   mountains   ~~river~~

1

2

river

3

4

2 **Draw a landscape from Activity 1.**
Draw and label four things you can see there.

Learn about features of natural landscapes

3 Read the postcard and write the words.

Dear Mark,

I'm on holiday with my family in Australia. It's fantastic! We are staying in a 1 _house_

in the forest. There are lots of

2 _____ in the

3 _____ . There are beautiful

4 _____ too. We can't pick them

but we can take 5 _____

of them. We can ride our 6 _____

every day. We can ride horses too. It's really fun!

See you soon,

Hugo

4 Read again and write *yes* or *no*.

1 Hugo is in Australia. _____yes_____

2 Hugo is enjoying his holiday. _____

3 The house is at the beach. _____

4 There are birds and trees. _____

5 They can take photos of the flowers. _____

6 Hugo likes riding horses. _____

1 **Number the pictures in order. Then tell the story.**

1

The monkey gives coconuts to the shark.

2 **Imagine you are the monkey or the shark in the story. What do you do next? Draw a picture. Write about your picture.**

3 🎧 4.52 🐵 **Listen and colour.**

4 **Ask and answer.**

What are these?
Do you eat coconuts?
What do you eat for lunch?

What's this?
Do you eat fish?
What do you eat for dinner?

What are these? — They're coconuts.

What's this?
Do you like monkeys?
What pet would you like to have?

What's this?
Can you swim?
What do you do on holiday?

1 Look at the pictures and read the questions. Write one-word answers.

Examples

How many children are there?

_____ 3 _____

What's the boy got on his head?

a _____ hat _____

Questions

1 What is the girl with the
green skirt doing?
listening to _____

2 Which animal is next to the
flower? _____

3 What is the boy eating?

_____

4 What are the girls doing?

_____

5 Where is the spider now?
on the _____

Review

1 Play the game.

START

You're wearing a sunhat. Throw again.

You haven't got your sunhat. Miss a turn.

You can't find your sunglasses. Miss a turn.

You're taking a nice photo of your mum and dad. Throw again.

FINISH

They like playing at the beach.

She doesn't like the purple dress.

INSTRUCTIONS

1 Roll the dice and move your counter.
2 Say what the people like or don't like.

117

Review ••• Units 7–9

1 Write the words.

and   ans   at   ~~each~~   ed   ell   llyfish   oes   one   oto   ots   un

1

b

beach _____   _____

2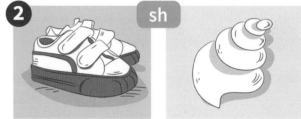

sh

_____   _____

3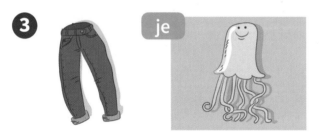

je

_____   _____

4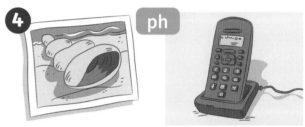

ph

_____   _____

5

bo

_____   _____

6

s

_____   _____

2 Read and colour.

This is Anna. Anna's wearing a red skirt and a big blue jacket. The jacket's got a black horse on it. She's wearing big purple shoes and short socks. She's got a big orange hat on her head and a big yellow handbag on her arm.

3 Read and complete.

1 He's looking in the `roimrr` _mirror_ .

2 She's wearing a red `rssed` _____.

3 He's taking a photo. He's got a `amacer` _____.

4 They're at the beach. They're playing on the `dans` _____.

5 He's cleaning his teeth. He's in the `rooabthm` _____.

6 This is a picture of our holiday. It's a beautiful `tooph` _____.

7 The fish are swimming in the `ase` _____.

8 He's talking to his friend. He's talking on the `oneph` _____.

9 She's playing tennis. She's got a racket and a `llab` _____.

10 She's at the beach. She's picking up a beautiful `ehsll` _____.

4 Read and correct.

1

He's ~~playing tennis.~~
skateboarding

2

They like playing basketball.
_____

3

He's dancing.
_____

4

She enjoys reading.
_____

5

He's wearing red shoes.
_____

6

They're catching the balls.
_____

1 **Write your favourite new words.**

Kathryn Escribano

With Caroline Nixon and Michael Tomlinson

Make a trail!

ruler
chair
~~playground~~
pencil
rubber
door

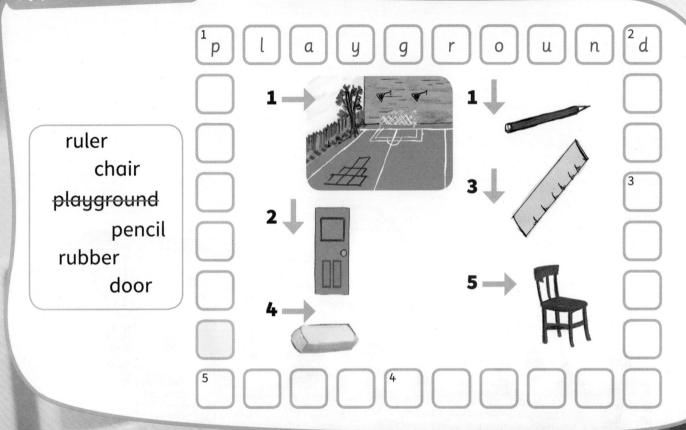

1 p l a y g r o u n d 2 d

Window to the World

These are classroom objects from now and from the past.
Which things are the same? Look and match.

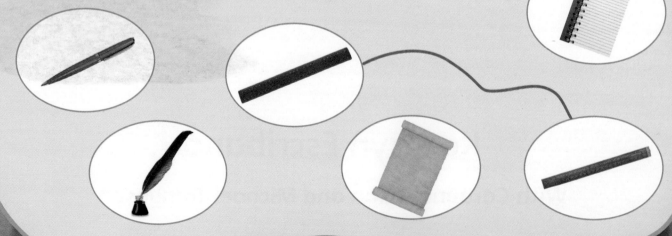

Where are the crayons?

Help Max find his crayons. Then tick ✓ or cross ✗.

1 The blue crayon is under the desk. ✓

2 The red crayon is next to the pencil. ☐

3 The orange crayon is on the chair. ☐

4 The purple crayon is next to the
    pencil case. ☐

Tongue twister

Can you say
this ten times?

red ruler,
yellow ruler

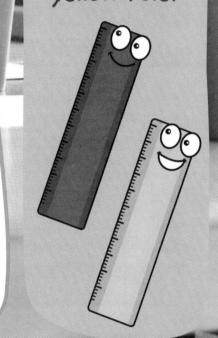

Home mission

Make a book with seven pages. On the cover of your
book, write 'I am' and your name. Keep your book.

1

2

3 I am ...

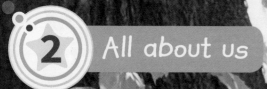

Family puzzle

family   mum   mother   dad   father
~~grandma~~   grandpa   grandfather
sister   brother

1. g r a n d m a
2. r
3. a
4. n
5. d
6. m
7. o
8. t
9. h
10. e
    r

Window to the World

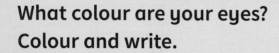

In the world, the most common eye colour is brown, then blue and then green.

What colour are your eyes?
Colour and write.

My eyes are _____.

4

The body game

- Play with your family. Take turns.
- You need paper, pencils and a dice.
- Throw the dice and draw the body part.
- When you've got a whole person, you win!

Complete the body parts!

nose

mouth

face

body

Home mission

Draw yourself on the cover of your book under your name. Write about yourself.

I've got brown hair.

Which is different?

1

2

3

4

Window to the World

To know how tall a horse is, we use 'hands'. This horse is 15 hands tall.

How tall are you in hands?

I'm _____ hands tall.

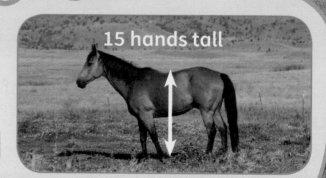

15 hands tall

Crazy animals

- Look at this crazy animal.
- Draw and describe your crazy animal.

This is a donkey-sheep. It's got long ears and a white body.

This is a _____ .

It's got _____ .

Home mission

Draw your pet or favourite animal on page 1 of your book, or stick a photo. Write about your animal.

This is my cat. It's got ...

Draw the mouths

It's ugly.

It's happy.

It's sad.

It's angry.

Tongue twister

Can you say this ten times?

soft sheep, sad spider

What's missing?

Look at the shopping lists. What's missing in the baskets? Draw.

bread
bananas
water
apples

grapes
sausages
chocolate
juice

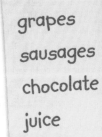

Tongue twister

Can you say
this ten times?

beans,
grapes,
beans,
grapes

Question time

Ask your family 'Do you like … ?' and colour the square. What is their favourite food?

Do you like bananas?

Yes, I do.

Name	yes	no	yes	no	yes	no

Window to the World

Some people use fruit to make animals.

Look at this animal. What fruit can you see? Circle.

apple   banana

mango   orange

Make a fruit animal!

Home mission

Draw your favourite food on page 2 of your book, or stick a photo. Write about your food.

I like sausages and oranges.

Toy sudoku

Write the missing words.
The same word can't be
in the same line ➡ ⬆.

radio   teddy   balloon

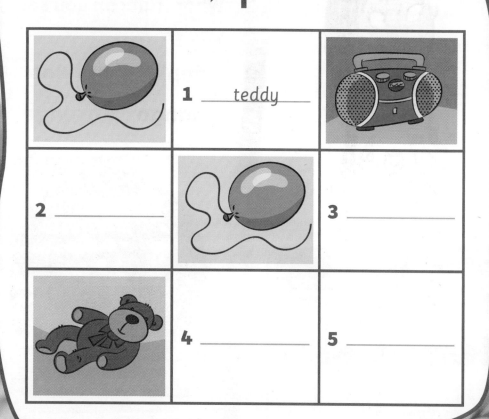

1 _____teddy_____

2 _____

3 _____

4 _____

5 _____

Can you say
this ten times?

sheep, ship
sheep, ship

Window to the World

Baby Sign Language uses the body
to describe things.

Match the picture to the toy.

Describe your favourite toy. Use your body!

a ball   a helicopter

Whose toy is it?

Follow the lines. Then (circle).

Max

Lucy

Tom

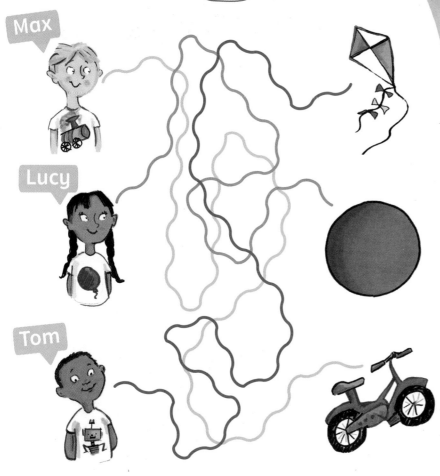

1 It's Lucy's / (Tom's) kite.

2 It's Lucy's / Max's ball.

3 It's Max's / Tom's bike.

Make word towers!

| d |
| o |
| l |
| l |

o l l d

a b l l

o b t o r

![Home mission]

Draw your favourite toy on page 3 of your book, or stick a photo. Write about your toy.

This is my helicopter.

Name the animals

Give these animals a name. It must start with the same letter as the animal!

Mike
Monkey

Tongue twister

Can you say this ten times?

Lucy Lizard likes lorries.

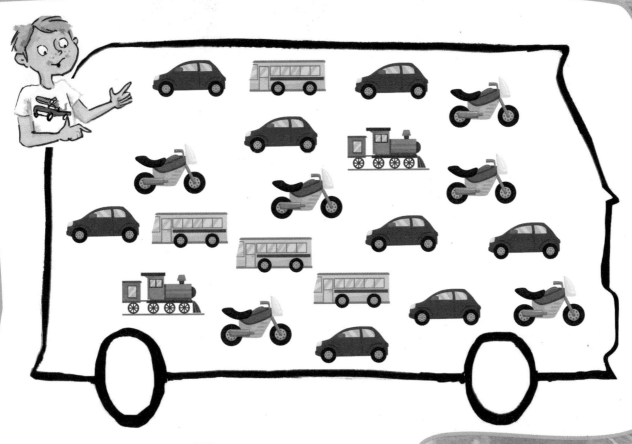

Counting time

1 There are [8] cars.
2 There are [ ] motorbikes.
3 There are [ ] buses.
4 There are [ ] trains.

Window to the World

Look at the photo of the Arctic.

Which animal lives there? Find out and (circle).

tiger   polar bear

hippo

Home mission

Draw your favourite place in your town on page 4 of your book, or stick a photo. Write about your place.

In my town there's a big park.

What comes next?

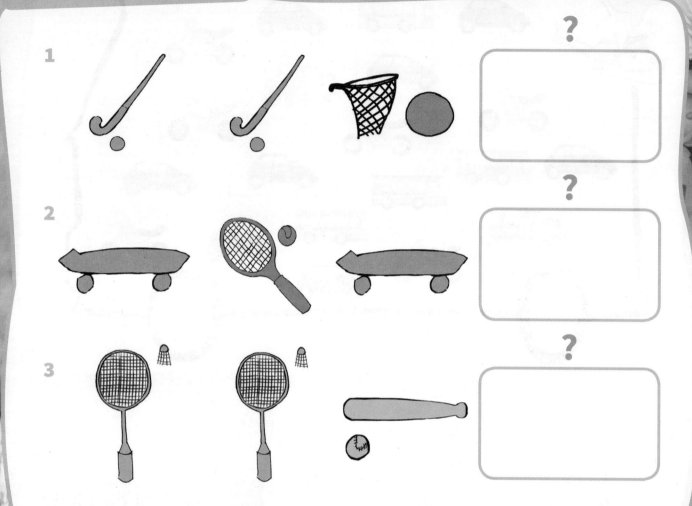

1

2

3

?

?

?

Make new sequences. Share them with your family!

Window to the World

Look at the Olympic flag. The five rings represent the five continents.

Colour the rings.

14

In the park

Look at the picture. Colour the answers for the questions.

1 Is Alex riding a bike? Yes No

2 Are Lucy and Max playing hockey? Yes No

3 Is Pat playing the guitar? Yes No

Home mission

Draw your favourite sport on page 5 of your book, or stick a photo. Write about your sport.

I like football and tennis.

House words

- Write the words. Use the letters in the box.
- Make a word with the rest of the letters. What is it?

a̶ a b c c d e
e f̶ h k l l m o̶
o o p s s u

1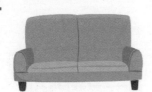

2

3

4

_____ sofa _____   _____   _____   _____

The word is _____.

Window to the World

Origami is the Japanese art of making objects with paper.

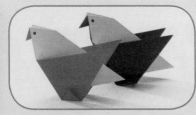

Make a paper house. Follow the instructions on this page.

Paper house

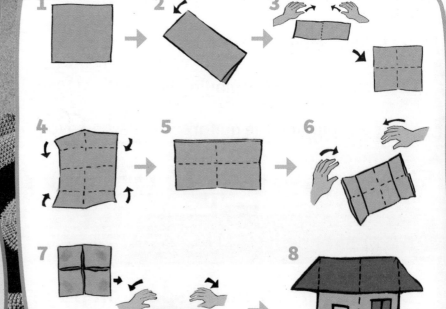

Lucy's bedroom

Help Lucy find her things. Then write.

doll **book** ? ? ~~pencil case~~ ? kite ? ?

1 The _pencil case_ is in front of the bed.

2 The _____ is between the bed and the rug.

3 The _____ is behind the armchair.

4 The _____ is between the computer and the lamp.

Home mission

Draw your favourite room in your house on page 6 of your book, or stick a photo. Write about your room.

My favourite room is my bedroom. There's a ...

Let's colour!

Colour the clothes. Use the key. Do the sums first!

6	8	10	12	14	16

shoes = 4 + 4   hat = 3 + 3

T-shirt = 8 + 8   jacket = 6 + 6

dress = 5 + 5   jeans = 7 + 7

Tongue twister

Can you say this ten times?

The jellyfish in jeans likes jelly.

What are they saying?

a — We like swimming.

b — I like playing in the sand.

c — I like picking up shells.

1

b

2

3

I like _____ .

Your picture →

This is the Doñana National Park. It's in Spain.

This is the Giant's Causeway.
Where is it? Find out!

Home mission

Draw your favourite clothes on page 7 of your book, or stick a photo. Write about your clothes. This is the last page of your book. Congratulations!

This is my favourite T-shirt. It's blue and ...

1 Picture dictionary

In the classroom 1

bag

book

chair

classroom

crayon

desk

pen

pencil

pencil case

rubber

teacher

What are your favourite classroom words?

In the classroom 2

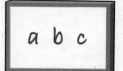

board

bookcase

cupboard

door

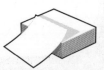

paper

playground

ruler

wall

window

Which things have you got at home? Find five.

20

Family

brother

dad/father

family

grandpa/grandfather

grandma/grandmother

mum/mother

sister

Close your eyes. How many family words can you remember?

Parts of the body

arm

body

ear

eye

face

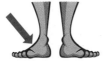
foot/feet

hair

hand

head

leg

mouth

nose

tail

Which three body words start with the letter 'h'?

Farm animals

cat

chicken

cow

dog

donkey

duck

goat

horse

sheep

spider

 Which animal has got eight legs?

Adjectives

angry

beautiful

funny

happy

sad

ugly

 Give each adjective a colour.

22

Food and drink 1

banana

bread

burger

cake

chicken

chocolate

lemonade

mango

salad

water

Which food from the list have you got at home?

Food and drink 2

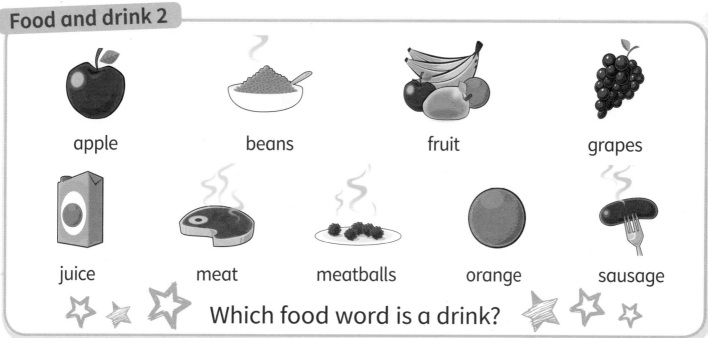

apple

beans

fruit

grapes

juice

meat

meatballs

orange

sausage

Which food word is a drink?

5

ball

bike

car

doll

house

kite

plane

robot

Which toys have you got at home?

Toys 2

balloon

board game

box

computer

helicopter

keyboard

mouse

radio

ship

teddy

 Close your eyes. How many toy words can you remember?

Vehicles and places

bus

bus stop

car

flower

garden

lorry

motorbike

park

shop

train

tree

How many vehicles can you see?

Zoo animals

bear

crocodile

elephant

giraffe

hippo

lizard

monkey

polar bear

snake

tiger

zebra

zoo

Which picture is not an animal?

Sports and hobbies 1

music

play basketball

play football

play tennis

play the guitar

play the piano

ride a bike

sport

swim

watch television

 **Which sports do you play with a ball?**

Sports and hobbies 2

badminton

baseball

catch

hit

hockey

kick

run

skateboard

throw

 **Which activities can you do?**

Rooms and objects in the house 1

bath

bathroom

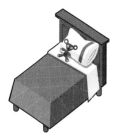

bed

bedroom

dining room

kitchen

living room

mirror

 **Which is your favourite room at home?**

Rooms and objects in the house 2

armchair

clock

floor

hall

lamp

painting

phone

rug

sofa

 **Which objects are in your house? Find five.**

Clothes

baseball cap   boots   dress   hat   jacket

jeans   shirt   shoes   shorts

skirt   sunglasses   trousers   T-shirt

Which five clothes words start with the letter 's'?

At the beach

beach   boat   camera   fish   fishing

jellyfish   sand   sea   shell   sun

Close your eyes. How many beach words can you remember?

Draw and write words you know in English.

Draw and write words you know in English.

Draw and write words you know in English.